JACK AND BILLY'S
TOP ADVICE FOR PUPPIES

Sally Bradbury
Steven Goodall

FIND OUT MORE

https://jackandbillypuppytales.com

Contents

Raising a Puppy

How to set your puppy up for success and avoid the pitfalls.

If you've read the book 'Puppy Tales: Jack and Billy' you'll know that Billy's family made a lot of mistakes along the way. It didn't mean they loved him any less, not in the beginning anyway.

At bedtime they left him in the kitchen shut in a crate from day one. He cried at night for a long time because he was scared and alone.

They taught him to pee on newspaper in the kitchen but then he got told off for peeing in the kitchen if the newspaper wasn't there.

They gave him lots of toys and left them on the floor amid the children's shoes and the TV remote and then got cross when Billy chewed the wrong thing.

They failed to socialise him with other dogs which resulted in him being fearful and then reactive when he encountered dogs. As a result of always being told off out on walks, Billy had little desire to be with his family and so when he was let off lead it was more fun to chase rabbits and squirrels.

One day he discovered a meat bone in the kitchen bin but not before he had scattered the rest of the contents all over the floor first. Poor Billy was often in trouble just for being a puppy. He did the best he could but he was destined to fail because his family didn't help him to succeed.

It's really easy to set your puppy up to succeed by just remembering these four points.

1. Prevent
2. Reinforce
3. Teach
4. Interrupt Positively

Prevent

Make sure your puppy doesn't become distressed and scared at being alone by taking them to your room at night or by sleeping downstairs with them until pup is confident enough to be alone. During the day, let puppy be with you in the early days if they choose to.

Put shoes in wardrobes when not on feet. Keep the TV remote out of reach. Use a puppy pen so that puppy is safely contained with his chew toys.

Reinforce

Capture behaviours that you like by giving praise and rewards when your puppy is engaging in desirable behaviours as this encourages pup to do it again at every opportunity.

Teach

Anything you'd like him to learn. Outside is where you pee; owners are fun to be with on a walk.

Interrupt

Teach a positive interrupter. Never get cross and risk frightening your puppy. Teach a word that means "Quick, stop what you are doing and get over here and see what I've got for you!" With the best will in the world no puppy goes through life never doing something they ought not to.

Think of your relationship with you puppy as a bank account. Every positive interaction is a deposit. Every time you scowl or get cross or punish you make a withdrawal. As soon as your account goes overdrawn then things will just go from bad to worse. Keep a nice healthy bank balance and you and you pup will soon end up as millionaires in the relationship stakes.

Toilet Training

Toilet training is all about creating good habits. Making sure that puppy is always in the right place when nature calls. Young puppies will need to go frequently especially when they are active. Puppy should be taken outside as soon as he wakes, after eating, after taking a drink, during play, before bed or a nap, if he wakes in the night, before you sit down for dinner, before you take a shower, during the adverts....

Billy's family made all the classic mistakes. They waited until he started to pee indoors before taking him out. This startled him and made him think twice about going when they were watching. Taking him outside after he had emptied his bladder was counterproductive. He didn't need to go any more.

They used newspaper on the floor and encouraged him to use it and praised him when he did. He learned to toilet on the newspaper on the mat by the door. He thought he was doing it right but of course it turns out he wasn't and he was then getting yelled at for peeing on the mat by the door. When they did decide to  take him outside all he wanted to do out there was play and once he got back indoors he needed the toilet. Billy soon learned to pee in secret.

Jack's family took him outside as often as necessary and simply waited for him to pee. Once he did he was praised, which along with the relief of an empty bladder, was a good feeling. Often they would play with him outside but only after he had performed and play always stopped to give him the chance to pee again before going in. They didn't expect him to ask to go out and he soon fell into the routine of going out at certain times and so quickly learned to hold on if ever they were a little delayed.

No puppy should be considered reliably toilet trained under about seven to eight months old. That doesn't mean you have to have accidents indoors, just that they are in training and if there are any accidents it is down to human error.

Puppy's First Walk

Everyone looks forward to the day when puppy can go out for a walk for the first time. Exciting times! But what about puppy? Is he as excited as you or is everything overwhelming for him. It's a big scary world out there.

Well before D-day...

Get puppy out and about in your arms or a sling or for car rides. Find somewhere to sit and watch the world go by. Let him see people and dogs and traffic in the distance. Watch for his reactions. Keep him safe, keep him feeling safe. You really want everything to be a non-event for him. Not too exciting, not overwhelming, definitely not scary.

People will want to ooh and aah over him. You'll want to show him off but don't let people overwhelm him. Don't allow strangers to approach him and touch him when he is in your arms unless it is clear that he is happy to make the first move.

Teach puppy to wear a harness and walk nicely on a lead well in advance of wanting to take him for a walk.

There are lots of ways to teach nice lead walking. Here is one suggestion:

At his meal times, walk around the house and the garden holding his food bowl and give him his food one piece at a time from your other hand any time he is there beside you. This is without a lead. Continue to do this until he understands the game and follows you about or walks with you for the whole of his meal.

Meanwhile use some yummy treats and sit on the floor and get him used to his collar and/or harness. Once he is happy to wear them and sit with his harness on for treats then attach the lead and give him a treat, take it off, give him a treat and so on.

Now, next mealtime, attach the lead to his harness, which he is now fine about. Tuck your end in your belt loop and do as you did before; walking around the house and garden feeding as you go. Voila! Puppy walking on a loose lead.

Keep those early walks with puppy short. Let him stop and take in the view, have a good sniff. If he can already walk nicely on a lead at home it pays to continue that lead training in very short bursts outside. Puppies don't need lots of road walking. They need to go on little adventures, somewhere where they can safely be on a long line and where they can run and play and explore then rest and sit and watch the world go by.

Enjoy your walk and make sure puppy does too.

Getting Puppy Used to Being Alone

The Flitting Game

By Emma Judson

There's a two-part game I call 'The Flitting Game'. We pick two adjacent rooms, ideally kitchen and living room.

Set your timer on your phone (silently) for five minutes. Then make multiple trips from one room to the next, fiddle with something in one room, and then move on. As you do this, ignore your dog – as in don't talk to him or touch him, but keep an eye on him. As he begins to settle, flit again.

Over the course of a few sessions you should find your dog becomes slower to get up, slower to settle, lurks in the hallway or in doorways, starts to look annoyed at you because this is now TEDIOUS... ugh! And unrewarding.

It's important to remember this is not some strict military regime, if you WANT your dog to come with you, to talk to him, to fuss, him, fine. Outside these sessions invite him along.

The point is that when you do not invite him, it might not be worth his effort to follow you. When he realises that, you can then occasionally add in a good reason NOT to choose following you.

So step two is to add that reason in – a big juicy bone, a big filled Kong, something that's highly rewarding and a pain in the backside to lift and carry around.

Now repeat the flitting, if he chooses not to follow you, try to stay a little less time in the 'away' room, a little more in the 'home' room, and build up gradually, second by second.

Don't always give the Kong or bone, carry on doing sessions without, and very gradually build up to other rooms and longer durations away.

At any point your dog is free to come and check. If he does that's fine. Don't say hi or anything but make a mental note that perhaps this was a step too far and so scale back.

The idea is that your dog learns that it's his choice not to follow and sometimes, that choice is highly reinforcing, sometimes it's just saving him some tedium and effort. He is free to check up if he's worried, there's no force or pressure at all.

Introducing a New Puppy to the Family Dog(s)

Introducing a puppy to the existing dog(s) needs to be done slowly and carefully while ensuring that they both get lots of one-to-one attention and that the puppy is not allowed to be a nuisance to the older dog. First impressions and experiences are going to shape their future relationship.

A lot will depend on how sociable the current dog is and his/her experience with puppies. Some dogs just don't do puppies. Occasionally an adult dog may be scared of a puppy.

Use stair gates in doorways or a puppy pen so that they can see each other without interacting and then you can be guided by how they react to each other. If you have more than one dog then they should meet the puppy one at a time initially.

The initial introductions may be successfully accomplished the first day puppy comes home or it may take longer. It pays to take all the time you need to ensure that nothing goes wrong.

Contrary to popular belief it is not advantageous to have the adult dog 'tell off the puppy'. It's not fair on either of them. There are very few suitable teaching dogs and those that are, are able to teach and guide puppies without using their teeth and frightening the puppy.

A new puppy needs to spend 24/7 with his humans in the early days and limited, supervised time with the other dog(s).

Always feed dogs separately and apply the same rule to chew toys or indeed anything that either dog may not want to share.

Happy Puppy Care

By Vidhyalakshmi Karthikeyan

Teaching your puppy to enjoy being handled is so important for their welfare.

Puppies have a lifetime ahead of hundreds of interactions daily with us, like having their collar and harness clipped on and off, having their nails done, being brushed, and having small wounds cleaned up and cared for. Even further, they are bound to need the vets or some medical care at some point. It is entirely within our ability to make all those experiences wonderful such that our puppies look forward to their everyday maintenance and care for the rest of their lives. Think about never having to worry about giving them a pill or cleaning their ears! Imagine if your adult dog asked to have their nails done instead of hiding when you brought out the clippers! Fear of handling is a thing of the past. The vet and the groomer do not have to be scary places at all.

All of that is possible through carefully structured, highly positive experiences. Every time you clip the collar on, give them a treat. Teach your pup to walk into their harness rather than you having to push it over them. Leave the clippers out or the ear cleaning solution open as you do other training or just go about your day to allow them to get used to the sights and smells of grooming equipment. Teach your pup that every single time you pick up the clippers, squeezy cheese rains from the tube directly into their mouth. It won't take long before they become excited when they spot you bring out your nail care equipment!

Ask a friend who visits you to help you with teaching your pup about handling. Ask them to touch your pup in the places where they already enjoy, usually starting with the shoulders or the chest, and feed your pup as they do so. Ask them to then touch your pup along the back, on the legs or peep into their ears for a second while you continue to associate each of those movements with great treats. Toss some treats away from the two of you for your pup to search and find. Wait for your pup to come back to you for more handling training. Keep it short. Quit while you're ahead.

If your pup hesitates to be touched, he might show it as follows: walking away, having ears back, showing the whites of his eyes, shifting weight back, excessive panting, pushing your hand away with his muzzle, growling or snapping. If any of these behaviours happen, stop and think why. Take things even slower and teach your pup that your hand simply lifting towards him predicts treats or play.

Also consider how you can break up whatever happened immediately beforehand into much smaller steps and turn that hesitation into optimism, usually by associating those increments with something totally amazing like squeezy cheese or a game of tug.

Husbandry training is vital for a dog. Having a pup is like having a clean slate. The more proactive you can be about teaching them that handling that goes beyond everyday petting is fun and something to look forward to, not just something to be endured until it's over, the better quality of life they enjoy as adults.

Introducing Your Puppy to a Harness

It's worth taking time to make sure that having a collar and/or harness put on, wearing it and having it taken off is a positive experience for your puppy.

Once they are happy to be touched anywhere, then introduce the harness. Have it next to you on the floor while feeding your puppy. If you use a clicker then you can click and treat puppy for looking at or sniffing the harness. Or you can use a marker word such as 'yes' instead of a clicker.

Once puppy is happily touching the harness on the floor, then hold it and have him touch it for a click and treat. The next stage might be to have him take the food from your hand that is through the harness with a view to him starting to put his head through to take the food from your hand.

Then pop it over his head. Click & treat. Take it off. Click and treat.

Make sure he is happy about the fasteners clicking before doing them up on him. You could even use the fastener as a clicker.

Some puppies will sail through the whole process; others will need it broken up into lots of tiny steps.

We recommend a harness with a Y-shaped chest piece for comfort. Fleece ones for extra comfort. Avoid using anything that tightens and causes discomfort. Harnesses with a horizontal chest strap interfere with shoulder movement and should be avoided.

Puppy Biting and Play

Biting is a normal puppy behaviour. Puppies investigate the world through their mouths. If it's within reach, it will probably be picked up and chewed! If it is exciting and moves fast it will definitely get bitten. Dogs play by using their mouths because they don't have hands.

Puppies need to bite and they need to play. What he is doing is simply trying to elicit play. Play is by far the best way to bond with your pup and is a great way to reward him during training so you don't really want to tell your puppy you don't want to play with him.

Don't get cross. Don't make noises that may startle or excite him more. Don't ignore him or use time-outs as this is time wasted that could be taught teaching him how to play appropriately. Don't just give him a toy to play with. If he's biting you it's because he wants to play with you not with a toy on his own.

Use tug toys that he can bite. Old knotted towels or a favourite toy with string attached. Unwanted dressing gown cords are ideal. You need to encourage him to bite one end of the toy while you hold the other end. Then you can have a great game together without getting bitten.

Ensure your tug toys are long enough and soft enough for your puppy to happily bite. Your toy should touch the floor while you are holding the other end. This allows you to animate the toy and keep the game low to the ground, so not encouraging jumping up. It also puts distance between teeth and hands.

Keep these interactive toys out of your pup's reach while they are not being played with. It will keep them more novel, which means the pup is more likely to want to bite and play with them when given the opportunity. Plant toys around the house and garden (out of puppy's reach) so you have them easily accessible. As much as possible, take the game outside.

Rotate chew items that you leave on the floor to also keep them interesting.

Do not play with your puppy unless you have a toy for him to grab. Don't let anyone in the house roughhouse with him or roll about on the floor with him.

Invest in a puppy pen for young pups so that they can be safely confined for short periods especially if you have children. This also provides a barrier that you can play through with a long tug toy before puppy has learned the concept of 'bite toy, not body parts'.

Start by animating the toy on the floor and saying 'getit' every time your pup grabs the toy. You hold on to the toy and let him grab it and shake it. Let go of the toy sometimes so that puppy is encouraged to come back to you to get you to start the game again.

At some point you can also teach a word for letting go. To do this you simply stop the game by putting a finger in pup's collar and keeping hold of the toy, release the pressure on the toy so that it becomes boring. As soon as pup lets go say 'thank you' and immediately invite him to grab it again with a 'getit'. He will quickly learn to let go when you stop playing in order for the game to start again and eventually the word 'thank you' (or your word of choice) will become his cue to let go.

Once your pup is getting the idea of the game then you can start to add in a 'sit' 'are you ready' before the 'getit' and before you know it you have a dog sitting and waiting patiently for the game to start.

Games to Play with your Puppy

Tug

Play gentle games of tug with your puppy. Use a long soft toy, rope or fleece is ideal. Animate the toy on the floor and encourage puppy to grab it. You just need to hold it and be part of the fun. There is no need to pull or shake the toy, let puppy do that.

Playing tug has many advantages; not least in giving him an outlet for his play biting. By putting it on cue you can teach a puppy what to bite and when to bite. Much better than trying to insist on no biting at all during play. After all that's how puppies play. They have no hands.

Fetch

Gently roll a soft ball or toy across the ground and encourage puppy to chase and pick it up and bring it back.

There are a hundred and one uses for a dog that retrieves. Perhaps the biggest advantage is that you can completely avoid triggering the guarding behaviour that is often associated with having to take an item from him that he has picked up. Something he shouldn't have. Using praise and encouragement just as you would with his toy will see him willingly bringing the forbidden item to you.

Find It

Let puppy watch you hide a toy and then encourage him to find it. Progress onto hiding it unseen and let puppy do what comes naturally and use his nose to search. Every family needs a dog that can find the keys.

The Lounge is for Lounging

How I manage to live in peace with a houseful of crazy Border Collies.

By Sally Bradbury

I have several dogs and very few rules but one that is very strictly upheld is that the lounge is for lounging in.

When we have a puppy I spend my evenings in the kitchen entertaining the puppy while hubby watches TV with the other dogs in the lounge. We do all our playing and training in the kitchen or outside. No toys in the lounge ever.

Over a period of approximately 6 - 10 weeks I can usually teach a puppy to settle on their bed in the kitchen for an increasing amount of time so that by the time the pup is 3 - 5 months old we can transfer that behaviour to being in the lounge. Of course it helps that all the others are setting an example.

In the beginning I'll be playing and training and teaching some impulse control and doing handling exercises: looking in ears, bit of grooming and this leads to some gentle massage and a settled pup. I might check Facebook on my phone for a minute while the pup is relaxed. A week later I might be able to reply to an email on my laptop while the pup is quiet on his bed.

We can then go and join the others in the lounge for a few minutes while pup is settled and this is gradually built up until walking into the lounge becomes the switch to settle.

I would never expect them to do this for longer than they can manage though. It is built up over several weeks.

Recall

Recall is less about coming when called and more about having a dog that wants to be with you.

There are lots of things you can do. Hand feeding, clicker training, playing tug or fetch, teaching collar touches and hand targeting, encouraging the dog to check in and reinforcing any desirable behaviours heavily.

Most important though is to prevent the behaviour you do not want, especially something that is so self-rewarding.

Long Line

A long line can be used to give a dog freedom but ensures they can't get into trouble, run away or get lost. Great for young puppies, dogs going through adolescence and essential for newly adopted rescue dogs. Always attach a line to a harness.

In a safe, fenced area the line can trail and when you want her back you either wait for her to finish running or you stand on the line when the opportunity arises and walk up it to her.

In an area where you need to keep hold of the line you will need to keep it relatively short. Let it out longer when appropriate and shorten it again if necessary. This is an art form so you should practice it in the safe area so that if you are worried she will pull you over you can just let go.

Hand Feeding

If your dog is not motivated by food outside then you can increase the value quite easily. Feeding her from your hand outside is a good way of getting focus on you. Start in the garden. Every meal time put her food in your pocket or a food pouch, go to the garden and feed a handful at a time when she is in front of you, wanting the food. Step back, say her name excitedly, feed. Repeat. She doesn't have to do anything except step towards you and want to eat.

Two or three weeks of this and you should be able to go to the field/park and do this at meal times. No running about if she has a full tummy just go there to eat and come home again. Then when you are there for exercise, treats can be used to reinforce her for being there with you.

Put her food bowl away and put all of his meal in a food pouch and hand feed her outside. In the garden to start with before taking it out and about.

Clicker Training

If she is clicker trained then you can click and treat any behaviour that you like. For recall I would click & treat just a glance back at you or looking at you as she walks past. You can throw her the treat and not even need her to come right back to you for the first stages. Gradually you would shape the behaviour into the complete recall and you add the cue once she's doing it reliably and of course mostly she gets dismissed to go again.

Playing

Toys can be devalued if she has them all the time. Let her have a chew toy or two and keep the favourites for playing with together. Tug of war is a great bonding game. For the most part play outside rather than indoors because this can make a lot of difference to the attention your dog gives you when out.

Pick up and put away all of the interactive toys indoors and at every opportunity take a toy from the cupboard and run out to the garden and play for two minutes. No playing indoors if you want her to want to play outside.

Collar Touch

Teaching a collar touch just means that every time you want to give your puppy a treat, a fuss, her dinner, let her in the garden, you take hold of her collar prior to giving her something she wants. This is actually a very powerful exercise and the result is that the dog will eventually move her neck towards your hand anytime she wants one of the aforementioned rewards.

Hand Target

Teaching a hand target is similar. It's easy to clicker train a dog to touch your hand with their nose and can be paired with the collar touch for maximum effect.

Teach an Automatic Check In

Teaching a check in and reinforcing desirable behaviours starts indoors. Set yourself a challenge. Put twenty treats in a pot on the kitchen side and every time your puppy looks at you (not when you ask her to) give her a treat. Count the treats left at the end of the day. Next day try and beat your record. Then take it to the garden. Lower your expectations for this. And of course then eventually out and about.

Premack

One of the biggest reasons for a dog failing to recall is because there is something better on offer if they don't come back. Premack is all about using the rewards the dog wants. Play with the dog, chase the squirrel, pee on the tree.... what the dog wants the dog can have, if appropriate, for checking in with you first or coming when called and is a good solution for the problem of what to do when she sees another dog.

Enlist the help of some willing friends with dogs. Arrange to meet someone with a dog who will appear at a strategic point, have your dog on her long trailing line. When she sees the dog stand on her line and the other dog will stop approaching as pre-arranged. Call her back to you. She can choose to stay where she is and look at the dog in the distance or come back to you and be released to go and play. It will take a few repetitions for her to learn how to earn the reward that she wants. You will need several sessions with several different dogs and you will also need to vary the rewards. She doesn't always get to go and play because it won't always be appropriate; sometimes she gets food sometimes a game with you.

Your aim is for her to see a dog and return to you when off lead eventually. This gives you time to ascertain whether it would be appropriate to allow her to go and see the dog.

Be Fun to Be With

Once you have added value to your attention, toys and treats, I'd suggest that when you get to the field/park, start tossing treats for your puppy to catch, get a tug toy from your pocket and have a game for ten to twenty seconds, then run about and have her chase you, do some collar touches, hand targets, whatever else she likes to do with you all still on lead and with the line attached (to a harness) as well. More treats, more play, drop the lead, pick up the lead, unclip the lead, put the lead back on all while feeding and playing. Do this for a minute or two and finish with lead off, putting toy and treats back in your pocket and tell her "off you go".

Whichever way she goes, you go the other way. Give her some sniff time, then start cheering and whooping and running again, get the toy and treats out again and repeat ad infinitum.

The one thing I wouldn't do when letting your dog off lead is ask her to sit and wait and then take the lead off and let her go. She'll spend that waiting time scanning the horizon and anticipating the release.

When you get to the field or park with your dog you want her thinking "Is she going to feed me, is she going to play with me or is she going to tell me to go?" When you take off her lead you want her thinking "Is she going to feed me, is she going to play with me or is she going to tell me to go?"

Retrieve

If a dog is bringing a toy back to you then you've got a recall. If your dog enjoys a game of tug then use a rope ball with a handle so he can chase, fetch and then enjoy a tug game with you. You can keep the game interesting by throwing the toy into long grass and sending him to find it with lots of whooping and cheering when he finds it and returns to you.

Chase the Kibble

Send him away by tossing a treat for him to find and more cheering when he finds it and a really yummy treat for coming back to you ready to go again. Stage 2 of this is to change position each time he goes away so that part of the fun is turning around and looking for you.

All of these games can be done at home, indoors, in the garden and out and about. On a long line or off lead where it is safe to do so.

The Do's and Don't's for teaching recall

- DON'T call your dog if they are busy and are not looking at you.
- DO call your dog excitedly when they are heading your way.
- DON'T call your dog back to you when you are walking towards them.
- DO change direction and encourage your dog to follow you and catch you up.
- DON'T chase your dog
- DO run away and get him to chase you.
- DON'T call your dog only at the end of the walk.
- DO call him and put the lead on randomly during the walk.
- DON'T ever tell your dog off for a slow recall. It will be slower next time.
- DO praise and reward your dog for coming back even if it took a while. Consider grading the rewards so that the quicker the recall the better the reward.
- DON'T use the line to make him return to you. The training is far more effective if it's his choice to return.
- DO use all these tips to make your dog want to return to you.

The Clever Stuff

If you have a dog that can recall perfectly unless... something puts a spanner in the works ... such as another dog, a squirrel, seagulls and countless other distractions then you may need some of our advanced recall tips.

Auto Check in When Seeing Another Dog

One reason for teaching a dog to check in with you is when you encounter other dogs. He checks in before being given the okay to greet. This ensures that all four parties, both dogs and both humans are mutually agreeable to the interaction before you release your dog. If it's not appropriate then you can reward him with something else and walk politely past. If it is, then what better reward than being able to say 'hi' to a canine friend. If your dog enthusiastically greets every dog he sees without checking if it's okay first then this will inevitably get him into trouble at some point and also lead to reactivity when on lead because of the frustration of not being free to meet and greet.

Teaching a Predictive Cue

This is done using a thrown toy (or food) for the dog to chase and adding a verbal cue. For this example we'll use 'TOY!' Over several sessions every single time you throw the toy for him to chase you give the cue. Now for the clever bit, throw a different toy (boringly to start with) and say nothing and then immediately throw his favourite toy as you shout 'TOY!' in the other direction. He should immediately be distracted from chasing the first thing he saw moving and go after the second one simply because of the power of the word 'toy'.

Teach an Instant Down at a Distance

There are various ways to teach this once your dog understands the verbal cue to lie down and it can often halt a dog in his tracks where recall has failed.

And Finally... If You Can't Beat Them, Join Them

If your dog enjoys chasing birds or squirrels or rabbits, have him on his long line attached to a harness and join in the chase with him. Chase the squirrel up the tree, the rabbit down the hole and the birds..well.. just chase them, whooping and cheering as you go. Be part of the fun and your dog will stay engaged with you and probably join in a game of tug with you at the end.

My Puppy is a Scaredy Cat...

The world can be a scary place for a puppy sometimes so it is important that we don't put him into situations that he cannot cope with.

If your puppy is scared of big, fat, bearded men in red coats then you can just keep him away from the chimney on Christmas Eve. Everyday things like the vacuum cleaner, the dog behind the fence up the road, visitors to the house, all the things that he will encounter most days, we need to help him to not be scared of them.

Constant exposure to something that produces a fearful response will ensure that the puppy becomes increasingly fearful and there is the risk that it can become a real fear or phobia.

Using the vacuum cleaner as an example. There will be two stages to this as vacuum cleaners LOOK and SOUND scary. We can start by letting puppy see the 'scary monster' in the room and giving him a food treat every time he looks at it or investigates it. When he is completely relaxed then we might push it or pull it a couple of inches across the carpet while puppy watches and enjoys a treat with each movement.

Before we plug in and turn on the vacuum cleaner puppy needs to be as far away as possible. In another room. You'll need a helper to turn on a stationary vacuum cleaner while you feed puppy a succession of treats. Over several sessions he'll not only get used to the noise and sight and seeing it moving but he will associate it with the food and positive feelings instead of negative ones.

Counter conditioning, pairing something positive with a low level of something scary is not about changing behaviour but about how the dog feels; his emotional response.

Learn to recognise when your pup is scared, allow them to retreat and watch from a distance.

To quote from Debbie Jacobs of Fearfuldogs.com:

"I hate to sound flippant when people ask what they need to do to help their fearful dog and I say, stop scaring them. Don't do things to them that scare them. Don't put them into situations that scare them. Don't let other people or dogs scare them. Just stop scaring them."

Preventing Resource Guarding

Preventing food guarding at mealtimes is easy. Allow puppy to eat in peace. If you have more than one dog then feed them separately and teach them that humans near their food bowl are always there for the sole purpose of adding a tasty treat to the bowl.

Don't be persuaded that you need to take your dog's food away or put your hand in the bowl while they eat to make them tolerant because you risk doing exactly the opposite and triggering resource guarding.

What is slightly more difficult when you have a puppy is preventing guarding of found or 'stolen' items. Puppies tend to investigate everything they find by picking it up in their mouth whether that be stones from the garden, the children's toys or anything that you left within reach. This is particularly relevant to gun dog breeds because they are hardwired to pick up and carry and always want to have something in their mouth.

By forcibly taking items from your pup's mouth especially if accompanied by getting a little cross with them for picking it up you are running the risk of teaching the puppy to avoid you, and when caught, to guard the possession that is now theirs and you are trying to steal.

The solution is to teach your puppy to 'give' so that you never have to 'take'.

To do this sit on the floor with a pile of toys and encourage puppy to bring them back after you have rolled them away. By sitting on the floor you are not tempted to move towards him. When he comes close while he is holding something, then tell him what a good boy he is while giving him bum or shoulder scritches. Do not put your hand near his mouth. Do not want what he has in his mouth.

He will probably drop the toy at some point and then you can throw it again. If he's a foodie then a food reward for dropping is a good plan. Don't use food as a bribe though. Only fetch it from your pocket after he drops the toy. Once he's happily bringing toys and dropping them in your lap or your hand add in other items, coasters, tea towels, anything that he might like to 'steal'. Then start working on him fetching stationary items as opposed to something you threw. Then generalise it to anywhere in the house. Leave things for him to pick up so that you can praise and reward him for doing so.

You should, if you approach this the right way, end up with a dog that will bring you anything he finds regardless of whether he should have it or not, while satisfying his need to find, hold and carry. Some people may consider it a chore to have your dog bringing things to you all the time but it's preferable to 'stealing and guarding' and it can be toned down later if required by only rewarding if you ask him to 'fetch'. If your puppy is already guarding 'stolen' items then it is important that you don't leave anything dangerous or valuable within his reach while you work on the above. If he does get hold of something then either let him have it if it's safe, or if it isn't create a diversion such as a knock on the door, scattering food on the floor or getting his lead out for a walk. This will only work once or twice though so keep that for an emergency.

If your puppy is already guarding food, resting places, toys or even you, then please seek professional advice from a reputable force free trainer or behaviourist.

Counter Surfing

Based on the premise that any behaviour a dog is rewarded for he is going to repeat and that food is a primary reinforcer, it makes sense to keep surfaces clear of food or the dog out of the kitchen to prevent him from learning to counter surf.

For the dog that has already learned to counter surf, teach an alternative behaviour.

Take a chopping board, a knife, a tin of hot dog sausages and a suitable container. Open the tin and tip the brine down the sink and rinse the sausages. Take out a sausage and spend some time carefully cutting it into small pieces.

What is your dog doing at this point? If he has feet on the worktop then just turn sideways, block his view of the chopping board and pretend he's not there. If he has all four feet on the floor toss him a bit of sausage. If he is barking, whinging, whining then continue to chop up sausage. If he stops, chuck him a bit of sausage. Ideally you want to reward the absence of barking not the cessation of it so some rapid fire rewarding in the early stages may be called for.

Continue to reward him for four feet on the floor and quiet. (note: You are not asking him to do anything and neither are you asking him to stop doing anything. All you need say to him is a quiet "good boy" when you reward him.)

Now hold off on the next reward and see if he offers anything even better. It could be to move away from the worktop, he might offer a sit or a down if either of those has a history of reward. Basically reward the behaviour that you like. The more repetitions you do the more he is learning what pays off and so when you are preparing food those are the behaviours that he will offer. You will need to reinforce them still on occasions once learned.

How to Teach Your Puppy to Lie Down on Cue Using Capturing...

or How to Teach your Hooman to Give you Treats by Lying Down!

Take your dog to the smallest room in the house. Take with you a pot of tasty treats cut up small, a good book and a coffee or whatever you drink.

Close the door and sit on the seat that is conveniently provided in there.

Have a treat concealed in your hand.

Read your book but keep one eye on puppy. When she lays down toss her a treat so she has to get up to get it. Go back to your book and wait for her to lay down again and repeat. Say nothing except for a quiet 'goood' as she lies down.

When she knows that lying down gets her a treat, and you'll know when she knows, then add the word that you are going to use. You say "down". She lies down and gets a treat. Now try it in other places but start back at the beginning again, no cue yet. She'll get it even quicker the next time.

Printed in Great Britain
by Amazon